WET

For Dave,
Thanks for
coming!!

WET

Toni Stern

Toni

CIRCLESTAR
SANTA BARBARA

Published in the United Sates
by Circle Star Press,
Santa Barbara, California

Library of Congress Cataloging-in-Publication Data
Stern, Toni, 1944–
Wet.
Poems
1.Title
ISBN 978-0-692-32877-4

Printed in the United States of America
10 9 8 7 6 5 4 3 2 1

Design by John Balkwill
Cover photo of Toni Stern by Jerry Rounds

For Jerry

We are great fools ...; say we:
'I have done nothing to-day.' What! have you not lived?

—Michel de Montaigne

Thin shanks! Even so,
while I have them—blossom-covered
hills of Yoshino!

—Bashō

CONTENTS

AT HOME

FARTHER OUT

At Home

HOUSEKEEPING

I have a keen interest
in the debris
that builds up
in the house,
especially
on the floor.

It's not that
I want to rummage
through the
vacuum cleaner bag,
I'm allergic,

but I do examine
the bottom
of the dry mop
with a certain
sense of awe.

This funky reverence
engages me;
bowing down
and contemplating the
reanimating nature
of time
on material
briefly stays
the pressure I feel
to create
something artful.

Greetings Issa!

Don't worry, little spider,
this broom
　　　is not for you.

DINNER'S READY

When I was fourteen and
In the ninth grade—curious,
Writers famously contemplate thirteen—
 Ah Juliet!
Fifteen and sixteen,
But rarely fourteen....
The lost year.

When I was fourteen,
I was surprised at being
Famous for a minute,
Because I'd rather have had
A dog than a boyfriend,
And said so.

Now I'd rather have this husband
Than a poem,
Which may explain
The lightness of my
Verse, and why I
Burnt the zucchini.

True Love

I asked my husband,
Do you like me?

Yes, he said.

I don't like myself,
I said.

With a gentleness
both dispassionate and
pledged, he replied,

I understand.

BLOOD TIES

Mind and body being wounded in equal measure,
the suffering was not great.
Though my face had been shattered,
like toppled dominoes,
and the upper mandible separated from the skull,
my brain was also battered,
mercifully stalled.

I remember the tree.
I'll never know if I hit it with my face,
or was trampled in the subsequent fall,
after the mare and I challenged the gelding
to a horse race
up the canyon.

Fade to black.

I was sweet-talked from oblivion
by two, sun-kissed couples,
calmly discussing my vital signs
in French.

Neighbors.

For much of 1993,
I wandered the ugly, rented house
in a long white nightgown.
When I needed to be driven somewhere,
I added a white shawl to my ghostly ensemble—
a cocoon with legs, an embryo.

The body lives to heal,
and in time it has, remarkably so.
My smile, a bit lopsided,
is not without charm.

Though I've never had the stones to race again,
there are times when, lightened by the effort
of accessing the backcountry
on horseback, I am made,

fleetingly whole.

Birds & Windows

Another bird has flat-hatted
into the kitchen window,
making a distinct, staccato 'thump.'
I can tell by the sound
it wasn't calamitous,
more of a glancing blow.

When they hit hard,
the birds leave a powdery residue,
their shape imprinted on the glass,
as if the window's been dusted for evidence.

Some are killed instantly,
others knocked unconscious.
I can't tell the difference,
so I place them in the shade,
away from cats and curious dogs, and
if we're lucky,
in a half hour or so,
they recover, remember they're birds,
and return to the sky
full throttle.

TURN OFF

How

many

lunatic

insects

drawn to

the halogen

lamp

have to

frizzle

before

I

give up

trying

to get

into

this ruinous

book

?

BENEDICTIONS

Nine days into her
two-week visit, our
eight-year-old godchild advises,
"Tata, it's time for your nap."

It's 3:07 in the April
afternoon and I *am*
a bit behind.

Daniel, here today as
he is every Saturday,
has altered his routine,
leaf-blowing
in the morning,
"para que pueda
descansar después."

Now, applying a nasal strip
across the bridge of my nose,
about to tuck in my earplugs,
I feel supported:

I will nap on behalf
of the whole, wide,
weary world.

POPPI

Poppi I'm sorry for being so mean,
for being allergic,
and keeping you clean.
For loving another
more than I loved you,

for all that my heart
was unable to do.

FEAR IS A ROOM

South of my throat,
Down the hall of my sternum,
Arcing inward.

In a rare moment
Of objectivity
I open the door:
Slowly.
Peer in.
Nothing.
Nothing at all.

That's what I was afraid of.

POTLUCK

I used to have sage,
Now I have rabbits.
Besides it's raining.

The One with the Gun

I ease out of bed
so as not to wake the dogs,
then hoist the air rifle,
preloaded and ready to go.

I've been practicing my aim, firing
at a yellow target bunny
painted inside the lid
of a Robert Clergerie shoe box.

It shoots high.

During the day
the rabbits are invisible—
a faint rustle in the thicket.
Dawn's a different story.

Perhaps the half-light gives them confidence.
Perhaps everything smells sweeter at this hour.
All I know is, it's six a.m.
and I might get lucky.

Because they are impossible to trap
in a Havahart,
I demonize the rabbits.
Premeditated evildoers!

TERRORISTS!

The truth, of course, is far from this,
but since it enables me to do
what *must* be done, I indulge
this self-serving fiction.

It's more to my taste than regret.

STUCK

a paean to aging

What the fuck!
I can't sit still
And I can't stand up!

Wordplay

I just learned what *plangent*
means—
now I want to use it in a poem.

Plangent.

SCARS

From boiling rice,
Love bruises along my thigh,
And the old, self-inflicted ones,
I've almost learned to love.

The Sunset Lanai

I'm thirteen. I'm wearing a red-and-white striped one-piece swimsuit, buttressed by a little pair of falsies my mom's sewn in. When I tan, the sun's rays penetrate the red stripes, but not the white, and all summer I've had a striped ass.

It's Saturday and the regulars are poolside. These are Hollywood people, drawn to the Sunset Lanai by word of mouth that my mother, the manager, will care for them, and she does. Mickey, who has a tricky stomach, comes by every evening for his Scotch and milk before he goes upstairs to the little penthouse and his wife, Irene. For Elmer, it's his daily dose of insulin. She's engineered a secret passageway off Eva's back patio that allows the boyfriend, living next door, to come and go as he pleases, when the married Philadelphian who keeps her is not in town. The other women don't like Eva, but except for an annoying fussiness, "Wipe your feet," I think she's okay.

Tenants are in and out of our apartment day and night. Walter, the handyman, is a big help, but my mom does most of the work, and is always tired. I don't help at all. I ditch school constantly, coercing Walter into phoning the attendance office, posing as the butler.

Barney Silver, a urologist, owns the Sunset Lanai. My mother worked in his office when we lived in the Miracle Mile, a creaky old neighborhood, half a block off Wilshire Boulevard. She would call home in the afternoon, "I have to stay late tonight dear," which meant I'd be eating at the Flying Saucer, the diner, two blocks from our apartment. A hamburger and chocolate Coke cost eighty-nine cents. After dinner I'd cross the boulevard to Thrifty's, sit on a stack of magazines and read Little Lulu comic books. "Uncle" Barney lives with his sister, Sarah, in the big penthouse.

The first six months we lived at the Sunset Lanai, we were in a studio apartment. Now we're in a two-bedroom. The picture window looks out onto Sunset Boulevard, and my mom's filled our patio with wicker furniture and glossy houseplants. A double-decker cocktail cart sits at one end; outdoor speakers, the other. Besides the pool, this is the most popular spot in the building. My father's rarely home. A salesman, he's gone for long stretches of time. No one explains anything.

The sky is saturated in heat; my hair, bleached by the sun, is green at the tips from the chlorine the pool man adds each week. Today I will swim seventy-five laps of the fifty-foot pool, up and back counting as one. By the time I finish, the sun will have disappeared behind the west side of the building, the pool lounges vacated. My mother will have started dinner, and I'll sit at the table while she stations herself at the counter, smoking a cigarette, watching me eat.

The Sunset Lanai is shaped like an amphitheater, the illuminated pool, center stage. Sometimes at night I'll go downstairs and sit on the edge, my "toothpick legs," as my father teases, calf-deep and distorted in the alien-colored water.

ELEGY

When will
your lover return
and relieve
your terrible burden?

Why is Amy Winehouse gone?
Surely we made room.

She was so small.
Five foot three,
not counting the beehive.

I watched her on YouTube.
Her eyes, unblinking and opaque
gave little away,
but her performances
were generous,
full of risk.

She reminded me of a snake charmer,
or was it the snake, as she dipped and sipped
from the plastic cup at her feet?

I've read that life for her
was a calamity.
Her father loved her though,
you could tell.

Amy Winehouse
is said to have said
she started drinking again
because she was bored.

Perhaps if she'd said,
"*Unbearably* bored,"
she'd still be here.

Boo!

I got a little high,
looked myself in the eye—

Yikes.

ONLY ONE

frog lives here, delicately
chiming his whereabouts.
A bachelor frog.
He has a magnetic baritone,
like Elvis.

I already have my prince
so I'm not going to kiss him,
but somebody should.

Instead of a lonesome soloist,
I'd have him crooning
to his sweetheart,
Antiphonious.

JAMMING

Ragged euphorbias
tall as a man,
weather this tight-fisted,
iron-poor land.
Pink floribundas
jockey for space,
poise and predation
adorn every face.

The heat and the wind
and the stiffening cold,
the drought and the drenching,
the dog growing old.

    I go naked, I get high
    beneath the perforated sky.
    I'm the one who lit the match
    and tossed it in the berry patch.

The blisters that callus and
toughen the skin,
the mercies and malice,

the sun angling in.

Sixteen Crows

I sling marbles in the direction of the oak trees
girding the house, where adolescent
crows congregate and caw, flaunting
    their numbers.

If I don't want to get up,
I yell at them in my Gena Rowlands when
she portrayed *Gloria* voice,
    'Get outta here! Beat it!'
They back off a bit.

In the afternoon, they
reconnoiter on the roof—their iridescent blackness
punching crow shapes in the
    etiolated sky.

Pumped, pompous, and preening,
they're our intoxicated, rowdy neighbors.

Here first, embedded in our landscape,

they'll picnic on us
when we're gone.

A Story

Have you had lovers you would please,
who seduce and then forget;
who once you love them they perceive
your loyalty as your defect?

After B,
I moved to the beach with J,
typecasting the leaden skies
and grainy green Pacific
as characters in *my*
fractured fairy tale.

J, twenty-three to
my twenty-nine and
unlike my other *amants*,
not a Hollywoodian,
I barely recognized.
How would I?

The French say,
in French of course:
"There's no such thing as love
only proofs of love."
I had no idea
what that meant,

but J held on
as I wised up,
and decades later,
marriage
is what I know best.

The incarnations,
realignments,
comedies and woes.

There you are!
Gravel crackling under truck tires,
heralds your homecoming.
Good.
I've been mining this vein of inquiry
long enough.

Why dissect a rose?

Lost

It's not the diamond ring I squirreled away
just before our last trip that haunts me,
it's the inability to find it. There's a difference.
I can live without the ring, but my ego
is wounded.

Nothing illuminates Time's indifference,
like the search for some missing essential.
Scouring my closets for the umpteenth time
feels demented, and I've become childish and needy.
My family's upbeat willingness to join
in this hellish crusade is chastening.

Women hide their jewelry all the time.
My mother hid hers.
One night armed men broke into our apartment,
stealing everything but the pearls she'd stashed
under the mattress.

Maybe I should call this poem,
The Anxiety of Ownership, or, *The Tyranny of Objects,*
or better still, *The Fig Leaf of Self.*

      • • •

I found the ring. It fell off the shelf as I
was taking down the Martin D-45,
in order to sell it to a player who's decided
he must have this gem of a guitar for himself.

One less burden.

Narcissistic Realism

"Don't cry, please don't cry!"
I wonder if it needs more red in the sky.
"Yes, yes," to himself he said,
"it definitely needs more red."

WET

Before we installed the ear-shattering
smoke alarm, I painted its white face,
including the embossed directive
not to do so, a color as close
to the natural wood ceiling as
my limited palette allowed.

I don't trust my memory anymore,
especially when I'm steaming artichokes,
so I've made this concession
to conformity and safety,
brightening up my compliance,

with the stubborn rebellion
of paint.

FARTHER OUT

THE HAWK AND THE SNAKE

When the red-tail flew off with
the gopher snake
snug in its taloned grip,
my companion sighed,
I just looked, and
in that moment
grasped sentimentality,
and its absence—
the way one
comprehends E=mc2, say:
recognition, then, in a flash,
gone.

The snake, utterly relaxed,
appeared reconciled to the
fullness of his predicament—
each scale a mirrored sun,

and then the hawk's fierce
eye.

Newtown Connecticut
the day after.

We only ever love our mother,
Barely tolerate each other,
Build a life,
Reproduce,
Convince ourselves
We've been of use.

· · ·

The rock stars are planning a concert,
The poets are writing a poem.
Each and every one of us
Forsaken and
Alone.

I Don't Like Her

It's shame I feel—riding
in the car with my mom and another little girl,
foisted upon me by her mother and mine.

"Look at this, at that," I sang out,
 as she, alone in the back seat, feigned sleep.

I never could rouse her, and my insincerity,
marveling at bogus wonders,
mortifies me still.

Bad Medicine

The physician's
wife sleeps badly,
dreams of drowning,
wakes—still
drowning.

It was a second marriage,
and she gratefully aligned herself
to her new husband,

his arrogance and
lack of mirth
she reasoned, befitting
his stature. Besides,
she was fed up with nursing.

    1993

    2003

    2013

An unexamined
life later, she
triumphs as a woman
of substance and sway,
in an anachronistic
bon ton devoid
of both—asserting,
and who could argue
she isn't,
living the dream.

Time Lapse

I gave the man holding the cardboard sign
ten dollars. It troubled me
I had nothing smaller—
then again,
I was driving to Goleta
to buy a fifty-inch TV,
and he was having difficulty standing.

It looked like the early stages of Parkinson's
complicating an already desperate situation.

In the seconds before the light changed,
he told me he'd been a war photographer
in Vietnam.
"I had fun," he said.

I drove away thinking how kind
he was to tell me that,
and at the next stoplight,
wondered if the sum I'd given him
might allow him to quit the off-ramp early,

and where he was going to sleep.

CAR TALK

♀ "Are we there yet?"
　　♂ "How should I know?"
♀ "You're driving."
　　♂ "Yeah, but you're steering."

♀ "Did you remember the dog?"
　　♂ "Of course I remembered the dog; she's back there."
♀ "What do you mean, 'back there'?"
　　♂ "What do you think I mean?"
♀ "I don't know, that's why I'm asking!"

♀♂ "Never mind."

Poem Courtesy of Netflix
Found on Paper Scrap

Yes, Minister

Yes, Prime Minister

Princess Kaiulani

Next Three Days

Divine Intervention

Time That Remains.

!

Has there ever been a more abused
punctuation mark, and doesn't it look
just like a vagina?
"I had a double latte this morning!"
"My child has a new teacher!"
"My name's Jennifer!"

Forty is the new twelve.

It's prosaic among these women's
twenty-something counterparts,
to go bald, or "wax Hollywood,"
as it's sometimes called.

Who's really getting screwed here?
The boys, led to believe that having sex
with children is the ideal, or the girls,
infantilizing themselves?

I'm for keeping the mystery of womanhood alive.
If our men want a closer look,
by all means—

They're invited.

I'VE GOT A PICTURE OF YOU IN MY POCKET

Walking down the boulevard,
head down, fingers flying.
Trailing behind you as if shitting them out,
miniature vignettes; holograms of those of us
you've acquired through browsing, then dropped.

Deletions of your mercurial mind.

Though obviously bitter, I admit your coping skills.
Everything's propelled by loss, and busyness
has currency here in the twenty-first.

•   •   •

Tu me manques:
My ease with languages,
Your magnetic sense of direction.

I think you think,
if you think of me at all,
I'm still here—

but I'm already gone.

Natural Resources

Always in a bit of a panic aren't we?
The animal urgency to look over our shoulder,
and the lengths we go to distract ourselves,
are breathtaking.

Peace is ephemera,
a fitful abstraction.
Dread's in our DNA.

In this winter of 2013–14
California's stricken,
a drought-ridden
Eden.

Edible California,
I am your homegrown daughter,
I fill my mouth with water,

bittersweet.

THIN

I'm thin.
I never realized
how thin
until I joined a yoga class
whose studio walls
are mirrored.

White women want to be thin, and I live in a white world.

"It's because you're thin,"
my husband explained,
as I considered why
some women resent me.

That was easy—
I always thought it was my hair.

In the mirrors of Mexico City, first thing
Latinas check out is their ass.

Thin has nothing to do with it.

HOLLYWOOD HIGH

It's because she would sing *Kansas City*
a capella, that I always associate Betty Garber,
the most popular girl in school,
with that song.

Even I adored her.

Three years later,
with their baby in the next room,
she shot her face off.
"I'll fix you," she allegedly told
her miscreant husband.

Dada di dada dadi dada da,
da di dada da di da.

THE MERMAID'S VERSION

My darling, my bliss,
let us tangle and twist,
the depth of your recklessness
launching our trysts.

I intoned where to kiss,
now you're genius at this,
the lush of your lips
in the rise of my hips,
the swell and the slick,
the quiet, the quick.

Imperious chasms,
improbable fits,
rebooting spasms—

Oh emptiness!*

*If ever forsaken, Nature permits, as grief's compensation,
your crew and your ships.

Tuning Up Is Music's Music

I've been Don Quixoting
the sweet spot, where
effort and repose
animate the present,
as long as I can remember.

Bugaboos of instability
dog my heels.
Ambition and the love of comfort
at odds, the moment I awake.

Awake?

The light has something to do with it—
and luck.

Whatever I'm pursuing,
here and not here,
I know I'll never attain;
that's the beauty of it.

Tuning up is music's music.

Six Large Glass Jars

Artists dipping into
the same river,

explain why there's
no water on Mars.

The sweetness in an onion
exposed to fire.

Waterproof boots.

Six large,
glass jars.

My mother,
my mother,
my mother.

The petals of love are
millions of miles from
the center.

The older I get
the easier I bruise,
which may or may not be
a metaphor.

I'm probably not
what you're looking for.

Girls learn that broken beds
bring the homeboys
to their knees.

In case of a surreal emergency,
break glass.

Empathy

January,
and the roses
    are shivering.

Because I Make It Look Easy

You sweep aside my feelings,
My need for love's display.
I won't try and change your mind,
You, who I hold so dear.
Perhaps I'll take it as affirmation,
As did Hamlet: the lost child,
And master of disguise.

The Oyster and the Pearl

"God, you're irritating,"
said the oyster. "You're like
a stone in my shoe.
I used to be more fun in bed,
now all I do is complain."

In the radiance of her heart
the pearl thought, "Poor oyster,
it's like trying to explain light
to the blind." What she said
was, "Are you kidding,
I'm to die for!"

ACKNOWLEDGMENTS

Deepest thanks to Candace Browne and Lesley Dormen for their encouragement, Bill Driskill for his poetic insight, Jerry Rounds for his love and intelligence, Trish Reynales for the terrific editing, and Carole King, my first reader, for believing in me.

ABOUT THE AUTHOR

Born and raised in Los Angeles, Toni Stern enjoyed a highly productive collaboration with the singer-songwriter Carole King. Stern wrote the lyrics for several of King's songs of the late '60s and early '70s, most notably "It's Too Late" for the 1971 album *Tapestry*. The album has sold more than 25 million copies worldwide and received numerous industry awards. In 2012, the album was honored with inclusion in the National Recording Registry to be preserved by the Library of Congress; in 2013, King played "It's Too Late" at the White House. The song also features in the Broadway show and soundtrack album *Beautiful: The Carole King Musical*. Stern's music has been recorded by many artists, from Gloria Estefan and Barbra Streisand to Faith Hill and Drag-On. Stern has published several illustrated books and has also enjoyed success as a painter, studying with Knox Martin at the Arts Students League in New York. She lives in Santa Ynez, California.

A Note on the Type

Wet is typeset in Spectrum, designed by Jan Van Krimpen for the venerable Dutch printing and typefounding firm Joh. Enschedé en Zonen. It was introduced by Enschedé in 1952; the digital version used here is based on the English Monotype release of 1955. Spectrum is a direct descendant of the great Aldine types of Venice, which are characterized by pen-based curves and oblique serifs. As venerable as its forebears are, Spectrum has a crisp twentieth century feel.

CPSIA information can be obtained
at www.ICGtesting.com
Printed in the USA
FSOW01n0131221214
4050FS

9 780692 328774